WHEN ANGELS ARE BORN

SAINT JULIAN PRESS

POETRY SERIES

Ron Starbuck's new poetry collection *When Angels Are Born* is a meditation, a prayer, a beautiful love song, an invitation "to sit quietly, in silence and in strength" and be transported into a world filled with light, where "we live inside one another" and where forgiveness is found. These uplifting and transcendent poems envelop the reader with grace and gratitude and echo these lines by St. Francis of Assisi: "All the darkness in the world cannot/ extinguish the light of a single candle."

We are urged to "live inside the mystery" within "infinite possibilities". Ron Starbuck reminds us "to become a sacrament of seeing," that "the mind is indeed a tremendous traveler" and "the heart is the first instrument of heaven."

At times lyrical and at times narrative, these are healing, transformative poems, suspended at the edge of the soul: "be at peace, the world/ and heaven await/ your surrender/ for each moment/ of your life." We are invited on a journey where "all the hardness/ of life simply diffuses/ like my breath/ into air." This is the voice of all creation, "you travel upon God's holy breath," invoking the eternal: "yours is a mighty soul,/ new as the earth was young,/ and or older still."

~ Hélène Cardona, Actor, poet and Henry James Scholar, author of *Dreaming My Animal Selves*

Ron Starbuck is my kind of poet – he writes with a clarity and simplicity that draw me into feelings and images that can never be clear and simple. His angels can be seen everywhere, but they speak of mystery that can never be captured anywhere. My favorite among his angels is his dog, "Nick," his "old friend" who "taught me the truth of unconditional love."

~ Paul F. Knitter, Paul Tillich Professor of Theology, World Religions, and Culture, Union Theological Seminary, New York, and author of *Without Buddha I Could not be a Christian.*

Ron Starbuck makes his poems from a very particular point of inflection, reflection and at times of deep genuflection. There are moments of lyrical beauty, of human intimacy shared with the stranger-reader that elevate the personal into the universal. There are also insights born of deep experience and transmuted into words and rhythm that gently and powerfully invoke the sense of the sacred. This marriage of emotion and spiritual consciousness makes this poetry especially memorable and helpful to the quest for the personal knowledge of truth that his readers will be urged more eagerly to make as they become more familiar with his voice and vision.

~ Laurence Freeman OSB, author of *First Sight: The Experience of Faith,* and *Jesus The Teacher Within.*

Other Books by

Ron Starbuck

Poetry

Wheels Turning Inward

Mark Miller's One – Volume 9
Wheels Turning Inward

When Angels Are Born

Poems and Prose Poems

by

Ron Starbuck

Saint Julian Press

Houston

Published by Saint Julian Press, Inc.

2053 Cortlandt, Suite 200

Houston, Texas 77008

www.saintjulianpress.com

Paperback ISBN: ISBN-13: 978-0615751498

Paperback ISBN: 0615751490

Hardcover ISBN-13: 978-0988944701

Hardcover ISBN: 0988944707

Library of Congress Control Number: 2013901881

Cover photograph is the image of an angel found within the Nativity and Epiphany Window, at Trinity Episcopal Church, Houston, Texas. Stained glass window made by J. Wippell & Company Limited, Exeter, England.

DEDICATION

To my lovely wife Joanne, who is a daily inspiration in all that she does and the people she loves, to our immediate and extended families, and to all our closest friends, both old and new.

TABLE OF CONTENTS

"Be patient toward all that is unsolved in your heart and try to love the questions themselves, like locked rooms and like books that are now written in a very foreign tongue. Do not now seek the answers, which cannot be given you because you would not be able to live them. And the point is, to live everything. Live the questions now. Perhaps you will then gradually, without noticing it, live along some distant day into the answer."

—   R.M. Rilke

Preface

Poetry is a language of deep intimacy, one that is meant to touch the human spirit and awaken it to the mystery of life, all life. When a poet shares with you the words they have written, you are being invited into a world that is intimate and wondrous, one that explores the depths of all human hearts. This is a world of openness and timelessness, a spiritual world that opens the eyes and ears of the human heart, and invites a person into the mystery of relationships and creation. We are called every day into a relationship with one another, indeed the reality we experience every day of our lives arises out of our relationships and the world in which we live, with all of creation.

Poetry celebrates this and offers us an opportunity to explore the mystery of human thought, interconnections, creativity, and design, our deepest intentions, in a *perichoresis* or divine dance of words, love, intimacy, and transformation. This is a spiritual indwelling, an intimacy, where we find that we do dwell within one another. The language of poetry is ultimately transforming and expanding, rich in rhyme and reason, in symbols and images, in myth, mystery and metaphor as each poem unveils a truth through the story it tells. A story grounded in humility, wonder and awe; the gift of love, wisdom, and grace that sustains our lives.

"Life is self-transformation, and human relationships, which are an extract of life, are the most changeable of all, they rise and fall from minute to minute, and lovers are those for whom no moment is like any another. People between whom nothing habitual ever takes place, nothing that has already existed, but just what is new, unexpected, unprecedented. There are such connections, which must be a very great, an almost unbearable happiness, but they can occur only between very rich beings, between those who have become, each for his own sake, rich, calm, and concentrated; only if two worlds are wide and deep and individual can they be combined. For the more we are, the richer everything we experience is. And those who want to have a deep love in their lives must collect and save for it, and gather honey." - Rainer Maria Rilke

We live in a world that undervalues such an intimacy of spirit, this *perichoresis* where we may get lost in the joy of our true being. In the joy of being together, lost in the joy of dwelling within one another, life, nature, and the whole earth, in creation itself. My deepest desire is to have us reclaim this joy, this divine dance, and the spiritual intimacy the gift of life offers us. My hope is that these poems will be music by which you will love to dance.

WHEN ANGELS ARE BORN

THERE ARE TIMES

There are times when I cannot tell
the difference between you and me, of
us together. When I see the beauty of

the whole earth because I see it
through your eyes. They are one and
the same as if we live inside one another.

We are as one as waves of light are
one, reflecting off the snow whiteness
of a jasmine blossom in spring.

We are one as light enters and bends
inside the inner surface of our eyes,
revealing all the colors and images of life.

Flowing faster than light,
swift as a thought, becoming a vision
held inside our sight,

a single white jasmine
blooming with light
in our neighbor's garden.

Through this light, I see
myself reflected in you,
of us together.

When you breathe in, I must
in turn breathe out. When your
breath catches the sweet, enchanting

smell of jasmine, my breath
catches too. You are the first breath
that enters into me each morning,

before my eyes open to daylight to collect
and hold in that light, before the day takes
hold of us in its hallowed breathlessness.

WHENEVER YOU WATCH ME

Whenever you watch me with the soft intensity of
  your eyes, places concealed within me begin to

open slowly, surely. You find inside me senses I cannot
  easily grasp; it is a mystery how with such a solitary look,

you uncover pieces of my being that ascend and
  open, to bloom immutably as sunlight opens

and warms the first soft white cherry blossoms in spring,
  whose fragile beauty and delicate texture compel me to

draw nearer, holding my heart entranced by such beauty,
  as your own spirit bids me enter into your softness.

We stand transformed by such splendor you know,
  resting in each sublime moment, like a monarch butterfly

before it takes flight, to land on that very same
  first white cherry blossom. Are we not the same?

IN PIENZA

In Pienza, we walked
down stone weary streets,
old with memories,

long before we were
ever born.
Your gentle hand in mine,

mine nestled in yours, in
complete comfort.
Our eyes

finding one another in a
home we had always known,
lost in hours outside of time.

Tuscan dwellings, ancient doorways
and hidden corners spoke
to us of ages ago,

of Renaissance Masters
who shaped a new world,
an urban landscape.

We were more than
young again,
moving as children

delighted with
a hopeful sense
of self discovery.

Seeing ourselves, our
dreams, gazing back
at us in each new face

that smiled and said "buon giorno".
Smiles that warm us even
now, like a bonfire burning

in the Tuscan twilight,
on Christmas Eve found
in night's dark resurrection.

In the stillness that finds
a Christ child within a womb
waiting to be born.

LEANING FORWARD

whenever i lean forward
you always seem to be there

listening, waiting for the sound
of my voice

there is something in you
that sees clearly the things

that even i cannot
see about myself

in our conversations we both
lean in, moving inward towards

one another, as if it were a sin
to miss a single word

one of us might say,
an utterance

even when we are apart
i can hear you clearly

calling my name
i always answer

SOMETIMES

sometimes it happens
this way

all the doors open
and lucidity

comes flowing
through

like light streaming
through a window

in this openness
each word and verse

comes together
without effort

without trying too hard
sometimes the world

does make sense
and leaves you in wonder

sometimes humility
touches us like

the softest feather
of a dove

in peace
in tranquility

and you ask
yourself

where will I
fly to next

yes, it is exactly like
this sometimes

and when it happens
gratitude arises

into the highest heavens
to dwell within this mystery

shining all of creation
back upon the self

STAY

Stay, please stay, as the night
whispers of
its tenderness.

Stay, and listen to our many
nameless
songs that hum in ocean swells.

So rich with unseen secrets,
with wisdom
found inside midnight all afire.

A radiant brightness
dancing within
each wave and flowing water.

May we flow
together
in this night,

wedded as we are in thought,
in purpose,
in bright hope, in high passion.

Seeing through another's
sight reveals
our truest promise.

Words turn into poems,
becoming songs
we share in confirmation

amid the constellations.

THE MONARCH
(Anam Cara)

Landing lightly she came as a revelation, a benediction,
   enfolded in the rich ginger and auburn of her Monarch wings.
     A mystery whose color I cannot clearly disclose or discern,

reminding me of a near friend, whose most intimate looks and gestures
   are a language unto her own, one we share in wonder filled moments
     together. Uncovering veiled places, which can never be denied,

as time releases a newness that cannot easily be named
   or found in all the known colors of this earth. In the Monarch's
     flight, she binds us together softly

upon wings that barely touch, so delicate in appearance
   and beauty they simply break open our own hearts revealing
     their truest majesty. We have learned to be brave together,

fearless in spirit, in a garden held independent of time.
   She takes my breath, folding it into her own with the
     brightness of her being.

And of us together, giving us breath, as we dwell in
   one another, as one body in one motion. In the
     delicate flow of the Monarch's wings,

in her softness, her gentleness, as she
   opens to me. Is not each star a witness to this
     unity? I love the color and shape of her eyes,

and how they capture mine, and how I see a reflection
   of her always in me, waiting like spring, when the milkweed
     blossom opens itself as a mystery to the first Monarch.

On the Butterfly and Anam Cara

In this poem, the poet intentionally blurs, mirrors, and merges the butterfly and the person together, leaving you wondering, which lines are describing either one. They may often seem like they are the same, breathing together with the same breath. The butterfly in many cultures and faiths is a symbol of the soul, the human psyche, and of an emerging consciousness, symbolic of immense spiritual growth and transformation. We may find a reflection of ourselves in both the monarch butterfly and those who we are closest to in this life. Here the butterfly as soul and spirit is touching on the healing and transformative power of friendship and love.

In Christianity, the butterfly is a symbol of the resurrection, as it disappears into its cocoon, into stillness, silence, and darkness, to emerge later wholly transformed, more beautiful and spiritually evolved than before. In this, the butterfly is a symbol of God's grace, even tenderness. It is seen especially around Easter, as a symbol of hope and love, and the power of transformation in our lives. It also draws upon language found in Christian Liturgy that sees Christ and the Holy Spirit dwelling within us all, and a spiritual indwelling within one another, Perichoresis; "be filled with thy grace and heavenly benediction, and made one body with him, that he may dwell in us, and we in him. (BCP – Rite I)" "That they all may be one; as thou, Father, art in me, and I in thee, that they also may be one in us (John 17:21)."

On the Anam Cara and the power of friendship: John O'Donohue (Irish Poet and Priest) - "The anam cara was a person to whom you could reveal the hidden intimacies of your life. This friendship was an act of recognition and belonging. When you had an anam cara, your friendship cut across all convention and category. You were joined in an ancient and eternal way with the friend of your soul." The term was greatly popularized by his bestselling work of the same name, Anam Cara: A Book of Celtic Wisdom, HarperCollins, 1997, p. xviii.

The Monarch is a poem about two such friends, kindred spirits, soul friends. Our own life may intersect the life of another at any time in a moment of spiritual intimacy and sincere friendship that is transcending and transforming, that takes us beyond the boundaries of our everyday self, pointing us towards a higher self, and the unlimited infinite potential of the self. Such friendships and encounters, even short ones, are to be valued for what they are in that moment, a gift from the heavens.

THE JASMINE BLOOMS

The jasmines are blooming, and tonight under
a full moon each blossom will be embraced in moonlight.
Their fragrance more than enticing, hypnotic, soothing,

with an allusion to some mystery that lingers and is then
forgotten from a garden long ago. There is something
you said, a question you may have asked, a song we sought

together in silence. Are you the flute and I the player, or is
this a song shared together? In notes entwined in deepest
intimacy, in conversations, in time where time is lost

in breathlessness. One desire fades, while many more call,
as you call out to me. Come forth, and let us dance this
dance of many beginnings. Let us dance together

with each constellation and in our dancing heal one world
after another across ten billion worlds or more within
eternity. Holiness, wholeness is one human heart

in harmony with another, in certain unity held
within creation, in worlds
without end.

THE CONVERSATION

I know there are many things left
unsaid, and questions yet not asked,
time will tell all, reveal all.

And the mystery that is you
that is I and the strength and
spirit of us when we are together,

or apart will begin to
unfold graciously, patiently,
lovingly in complete wholeness.

As if from the first point of creation
when time released itself from captivity,
where all things end and begin

anew in the nirvana out of which all
life arises. Where we learn with a
trust given by our own humanity

that we are the same as one
another. Where I feel the texture
of each thought

intimately sought that passes between
us as the moon knows the reflection of its
own light passing through the heavens.

WEAVE

Become what you weave, even now
you are woven together reed by reed,
you are the master weaver of yourself.

We have more questions than answers,
but the questions are wise? Must we not
ask first, before knowing?

Like the self, the wind has no name,
and it has many, whom the self is coming
and going, changing with the wind from moment

to moment. Our selves are many, they are
legion, they move through the wheel of life,

samsara, time after time. What is time except
an abstraction of the mind, an illusion only,
one we may come to understand? Let us ask

wise Vyasa or Ganesha, do you not think even
they would know? There is always a story within
a story, a tale within a tale. What do they teach?

Let us look toward the shining archer Arjuna,
Vishnu the unbeatable, unblemished friend
to Lord Krishna.

Did not creation burn from within Krishna?
Yet, in his wisdom was he, not a trickster too?
What can we know and discover from the ancients?

To look within, as did the Buddha or Christ,
to empty the self, let go of all suffering and
desire, is not this wisdom?

Only in the silence and stillness of time, beyond
all time, may time redeem time itself and the soul.
Take one breath, and then another, is not all time

held in one breath? Does not the stillness
and space between each breath, transcend time?
Here is the eternal, let the heart be still,

let knowledge come. This is the path of wisdom,
letting go. Being and becoming, the self knows
this, it is written, weave away with bamboo and

bark, with a cane or rush, with each silver thread
of your spirit gather in such stillness, beyond
all forms, formless.

Without fear or fault, with compassion
for the self, for others, saving the world,
this is the Great Perfection, Nirvana.

DOES CHAOS RULE?

Does chaos rule, or order,
are the stars fixed or moving?
It is a dance, constellations

spinning in motion as the soul
travels from one self
to another.

We are joined together in this
dance, moving in unity, as one.
We breathe the same air in

one single breath as creation
sighs in sighs too deep
for words or voices to describe.

Listen, here is the silence of
the Mockingbird between each note.
Listen, here is the silence of the sea

between each wave breaking
upon the shore. Listen, here is the
silence of each tree growing within

a forest. Listen, here is the self calling
out to the world as it sits in silence,
in deepest meditation.

Listen, here is the self composing
the song of life. Life calls to life,
it has always been so.

All creation groans in childbirth within
each moment of enlightenment, of unity.
Our awareness cuts like a sword through

each thread of illusion woven from a
dark veil. We see only in part until
we are fully known. Each relationship

a treasure parting the veil. We make this journey
together, we dance as one, we breathe together
as one with all creation.

LAUGHTER IS ITS OWN HEALING

Laughter is its own healing,
one that turns our
world around.

May we speak of desire,
of joyfulness, pleasure
and delight?

The white jasmine's scent tickles
my nose, its blossom pleases the eye,
revealing something hidden

within. Is not this true for you?
A hand reaches out to caress a
face an aspect, while a thousand

neurons arouse the brain. Ah,
the body-mind knows this pleasure,
the pleasure of another's

touch. And the heart, what does
the heart know, the seat of wisdom?
It is good to love. When it beckons,

let us follow with pleasure and
come to know one another.
Whom may I touch today?

Whom may I love once more? How
will I share my life? Life calls, life
calls out to life beyond the chaos.

When my desire turns from joy to
sorrow as it will, let me embrace
it with my whole life accepting chaos.

Between joy and sorrow
there is an endless balance,
a resting mindfulness.

In this passing and accepting we
find our truest ecstasy, in perfect
love we find no fear.

IN A NAMELESS CITY

In a nameless city, a radical fundamentalist sits nervously
before me with a cup of coffee in hand. Trying to explain
to me the absolute reality of his beliefs, his truth, his god.

Don't bother to ask me which beliefs, it hardly matters,
they're his own. I try to remind him how extensive
the visible universe is, how old and open that what

we see from earth is 28 billion parsecs in diameter. How
small we all are in such a vastness. I try to explain that what
we do see is only a partial vision

of the eternal, arguing creation is boundless. And when
seen from inside God's eye, how it is always expanding
in its acuity as his sight moves effortlessly across creation.

How the known universe is always changing, growing,
evolving even as we speak; as a mystery. And the best
we can do is live inside this mystery,

when what we do know is only a single grain of sand resting
with a finite number of other grains. What we know
is that our billions of galaxies far out number

all the grains on all the beaches humankind ever walked
upon through human history. I try to tell him how
precious and unique all life is, how sacred.

How we are, meant to love and be loved. His eyes are blank.
I say all this to him while looking directly into each one of
his blue eyes, trying my best to make some connection.

Then I see the vest under his coat, the look of fear in his eye,
words hurriedly spoken to an unknown god come spilling out
of his mouth in a travesty of prayer, an explosion of light and heat.

Then the utter silence of many voices, which will never
be heard again. The silence deafens us.
It is death.

SANDBURG & MONROE
(The Visit 1961)

The photographs nearly say it all
  you know, what can another poet

add to these moments of
  intense intimacy between

two spirits, two hearts. The wise old poet,
  filled full with his life, with his memories.

With his words and songs that
  stopped a nation dead in its tracks

more times than I can count now.
  Who was more than a country's conscience,

who could turn a phrase, a verse
  and help us to see the

pain, and beauty, and joy
  within life clearly.

Who lifted a nation up on his own
  broad "Big Shoulders", and told us,

we were better than this, or better than that,
  better than we thought at least, or ought to be.

A world of dreamers, and the builder
  of such dreams, undreamt of in our imaginations,

breathing in fully the smoke and opiates of a whole
  lot of dreamers, who keep daring to dream.

And then there is Marilyn or Norma Jean,
  an icon to the mid-twentieth century,

wrapped up in soft, innocent sexuality, and vulnerability.
  There's not a man dead or alive today

who can resist her haunting beautiful looks.
  Our desire, you see, runs full force with her, but

with some tenderness and compassion we feel for any child
  who has fallen and scuffed their knee.

She, in the enigma that was uniquely her, fell many
  times, a riddle to more than one man.

Still, when you look closer, delve
  deeper, there is something more

there than sorrow and misuse. A searching
  intelligence, a poem perhaps, waiting

at the edge of her soul, suspended at tongue tip,
  a voice she never discovered to speak with clearly.

I wish we could give her that writer's voice
  now, to let it converse in all its elegance.

Sandburg saw it, he saw her (Monroe) more clearly
  in this moment than all the

movie directors and producers who ill-used her,
  counting up coins in their film editing rooms.

He saw, I think, another poet begging to be born,
  a new voice waiting in discreet misery to breakout.

Someday soon, we must ask ourselves, more than once
  I think, about the high price we place, or don't, on great art.

Whatever answer you give, she paid it
  tenfold and more I believe,

and we, we are the poorer, the losers who never
  heard her truest voice.

Sandburg knew what this day meant to her, she became
  more alive in his gentle and reassuring presence

than any film might have captured. And Marilyn,
  I believe, found some peace and joy then too.

In the simple act of living, of being herself with other people,
  which it seems she rarely found in her short life.

Wherever they are in this world today, together perhaps
  in another life and another time,

I hope they are holding one another with the same
  tenderness and intensity seen here, in an old photograph

that captures their spirits once more. At least, that is what
  I would wish, imagine for them both.

Two souls, bound together within time and outside of time,
  in a timeless moment held beyond eternity.

YOUTH & REBELLION

Do you remember
the days of your childhood?
of summer nights
of grand adventures

of flying to the moon
and back again
of running and jumping for joy
of PF-Flyers and Kids

with which you
traveled all over your world

of being a kid without any worries
of a home safe and sound
and the joy found there
when the world was right

when innocence was known
and never lost
and never lost

and the simple pleasure of our
childhood days, of wonderment and curiosity
that may have killed the cat, but never you
when imagination knew no bounds and

everything you did was an opening up
to the mystery of life, to life itself
to the friends
we found and lost.

"to ginger and spice and everything nice,
to snakes and snails and puppy dog tails"

and the red headed girl who
lived down the street
who captured your heart
with all of her charms

to lightning bugs
who guided us home
and guide us still
and guide us still

RAIN DOWN UPON US SOFTLY

when i think of you, it is
  with a breathlessness

that goes beyond all knowing
  beyond each heavenly muse

you are my muse, my ancient heart
  to transform the world

i could wish for the stars
  to rain down upon us softly

for their light to
  enter every cell

turning the mind
  brightly

for the body to rejoice,
  with pleasure

in their light, in
  your softest touch

your breath, as it
  mingles with mine

as each star
  shines out of the night

then when the morning
  comes, fade from the sky

as some sacred part of us
  aches for their return

for one another, a simple touch,
  a glance, a loving look

may the night cover us
  again and again, in a sea of stars

spread out across
  the milky way

where we may lay down
  in mystery together

where all the memories
  of humankind

are stored,
  named

as constellations, each single one
  a loving token to the heavens

as i remember the touch
  of your hand on mine

and a look that sees
  beyond all possible realities

ANGELS WEEPING
(The Culture Wars)

blood is everywhere
  unseen perhaps

intentionally not noticed
  but if you are mindful today

you will taste it in your mouth
  like a steak served medium rare

let's sharpen our teeth today
  on one another

on the bones of memory
  and the fear we eat

a dark sacrament of flesh, shut off
  from one another as we are

here take another bite please,
  as you choke on all that bitterness

is the wish to kill never killed,
  where is forgiveness found

i'll hand you my next pound of
  flesh, lost in an argument of words

can you see the angels weeping,
  their cheeks warm with sorrow

I wish we could taste their tears,
  to return us to some form of sanity

THE BUDDHA SPEAKS (FIRE SERMON)

the Buddha speaks
his flaming tongue trembles
with fire in every word

the world burns
with desire after desire
with clinging

to things, of which
there is no need
with hatred

and disenchantment
that offers no rest in
heaven or earth

all is burning within us
our tongues
our ears

our nose
our eyes
the mind

the body
itself
burns

what i want to
share now is to let
your heart burn brighter

with a greater desire that
goes beyond all universes
beyond all thoughts

to save the self
beyond the self
beyond all suffering

beyond the mind
that never stops
let compassion

rule the mind
let it arise
from the center

of yourself, from
the heart, where
all silence is known

where stillness rests
where each moment
is born anew

where dispassion
is known, in a
passionate embrace

where all liberation rests
in the heart's core, where
we see with a wisdom

marked by certainty
as did the Buddha
as did Christ even

in his darkest hour
let go of suffering
let go and be

let the openness of
all creation empty you
of all desires

to understand in
a moment's thought
that what you truly are

is the truth of all creation
woven together
thread by thread

being by being
be at peace, the world
and heaven await

your surrender
to each moment
of your life

OPENNESS

There is an openness to
  all creation we are just
beginning to understand.

Each thought, each word
  we utter from the stillness
of our hearts,

echoes across the landscape
  of life, creating new realities,
infinite possibilities.

Where the mystery dwells within,
remembers.

We are the author, the poet,
  the music and the song which
opens up to you O, Lord.

We are the singer in the dream,
  the dreamer within the dream, giving
birth to every moment.

We are your heart's blessing, born
  of love, that saves uncounted worlds
across uncounted universes.

Where the mystery dwells within,
remembers.

DESIRE NEVER FADES

When you are old and gray and full of sleep,
And nodding by the fire, take down this book... W.B. Yeats

it's not that desire
  ever fades, even with age
    i remember well the

softness of your eyes
  their deep look,
    looking back at mine,

a yearning touch,
  soft and gentle
    as down,

urgent and immediate,
  burning fiercely, sultry
    breath as we

inhaled together, blended
  as one, no one has such
    warm hands and soft lips

time all
  arrested,
    in such a moment

falling freely together
  an intimacy of spirit
    one soul speaking, while

the other answers, more deeply
  than all the waters of earth
    that run

back into the source
  of life, i remember
    each sacred moment

of holding you, of gazing
  into the brightness of your eyes
    and i remember too, the call

of passion, one self to another
  lost in an ardor that longs only
    for the other's touch

it never dies you know
  desire, love, name it
    what you may wish now

it lives on, always
  to warm us with memories
    in the wonder of winter

in the warm memories of you
  my dearest one, who touches
    me deeper than words may say

DANCING LIKE LIGHTNING

As a child, and even now
  I loved lightning storms
rolling in across the prairie

or the high desert mesas,
  or even in from the Gulf
of Mexico, rushing across the water

tell me please, have you
  ever wanted to dance
like the lightning does

coming down from the heavens
  to prevail in the middle of a great storm,
to be filled with such a strength

imagine if you will
  what this dance would be like
you are the lightning

you are the starting point
  the single white point, that turns
and in that turning

whirls about and pirouettes
  to flash and burst
across the undulating sky

streaking from cloud
  to cloud and then
between each rain drop

between the rain gods and the thunder gods,
  between the hail gods and the ice gods,
who are actually

more like angels moving
  between accelerating electrons
to seed the sky

you are the electrical discharge
  the super heated air, expanding
rapidly, the shock wave heard as thunder

in the darkness of the storm
  you are the only source of light
that touches both heaven and earth

you are the center of
  the storm in all its majesty
and in all its might

that brings the rain
  to both field and garden
feeding the whole world

think about this please
  if you could live your life
with such a power and purpose

what would that look like to you
  when would you begin, tomorrow, today,
in an hour, this very moment

now perhaps?

PARK AVENUE

Here, I am with my
 begging bowl in hand,
that only I can see.

I am in the heart of Manhattan,
 dressed in a Canali double breasted suit
walking from St. Bart's to the

Waldorf, it's only one block and
 a world away from home. A young
lady passes by, smiles and that is all it

takes you know, one solitary smile, and
 my begging bowl is full once more.
Such riches come rarely, such joy

is known as Shantideva teaches, by
 wishing joy to others first. Did you know?
That a single smile, like this one, can

save ten thousand worlds, across ten
 thousand universes, as if the first light
of creation has turned back upon the world.

THIS IS WHAT I KNOW

No soul, the self, is ever lost,
this I know for certain. The self
lives on forever, death an illusion only.

We travel through life as through
a dream, through time itself.
And yet, each moment a simple

measure by which we mark the passing of
our earthly breath. When all is said and
done of life, when alar angels and archangels

come to gather us back into our truest
form, found in eternity's royal reign,
God's embrace.

No soul, the self, is ever lost,
whatever you may believe
each thought ascends in stillness,

as silent prayers opening all the heavens.
Yes, there is more than one. Arising as
subtle memories, as a mist above the sea,

moving in one accord, they flow
inside the tides of heaven, in hallowed unity
with God's holy breath, spilling across creation.

Stitching memories together as sutras,
one thought after another, woven into
the holy cloth of ceaseless consciousness.

Imagine yourself, as being borne upon
each breath, breathing life into life,
creation's finest desire.

No soul, the self, is ever lost, gathered
as we are with gratitude into God's
bright memory, eternity unending.

Where each remembrance
shared is used to love and heal,
as life calls to the living.

This, O family of humankind, is
why we each are born, carried
as we are, upon the breath of God.

No soul, the self, is ever lost,
remember this, you travel upon
God's holy breath, a simple thought,

exquisite in its elegance.

AUSTIN DAVID MEEK

Since God is love, which is the very best way
mortals can imagine God to be,

then you have been surrounded by love and holiness
all your days and beyond. Yes, beyond.

If I could tell you the mystery of creation, I would say
it's within you my lad, grasp it clearly my lad,

it's love again my lad. You hold it my lad; in
all your tenderness and strength, you hold it near.

So, be the mystery my lad, keep on loving my lad.
And if we could speak, and somehow I think we can,

I would explain how God has known you from the
beginning of all creation, as a single thought and more.

Such is the mystery of being and love, of God's longing
for us all; it's yours my lad, take hold of it my lad.

If I could show how love works my lad, I would say
you are love in the making. You are a miracle

of love and faith, of prayer and hope. I would tell the story
of how you have bound together person after person,

generation within generation, people and souls you
may yet still meet within God's wonderful realm.

I would tell what a gift you are and continue to be
to family, friend, and unknown unnamed strangers who

prayed for your bright young life and dear old soul.
You are a blessing of God, a gift meant to bring us

home to ourselves in the wonder of it all; in the wonder
of life, of life itself, the gift of life.

You are a blessing that transcends us all, that God has
given us each in a unity of love.

You are more than flesh and blood and breath, more than
we may imagine or see, more than mortal form may know.

So grasp it dearly my lad, be proud my lad, lay it all
out my lad, then let it go with love's finest blessing;

because this my lad, is being my lad, the
gift God gives us all. You are that gift.

If I could speak to you of the soul, I would say
that yours is strong my lad, treasure it my lad.

Be glad of it my lad; yours is a mighty soul,
new as the earth was once young,

and older still -- as the stars above Jerusalem and
this ancient earth are older still -- than memory can tell.

If I could tell you of love's gift, I would say
that it's yours my lad, you have it my lad.

You are gentle as the breath of God's Holy Spirit that gave
and gives us being itself my lad, breathe deep my lad.

STORM SHADOW

Every day of my life I want to be standing in the
  shadow of a good clean storm, where the rain comes down so
hard and bright it washes the soul pure, to leave it gleaming
  and polished in all its tenderness. Where the grace of the lightning

reflects off of every rain drop.
  And then pours over the body like a holy baptism and sacrament
of faith that calls out in name to every saint that was ever born.
  Where the thunder awakens us to life, and we breathe in

everything of this earth that is good and dear, absolutely perfect
  in our many imperfections.
Where angels enter in without fear, to carry us into the
  still wholesome heart of God, beating in union with our own hearts.

Do you think you could live in such a way, where
  nothing else matters, except the flower of yourself opening
up again and again, and then wider still,
  to receive the blessing of this shower, as dark and loamy soil,

where our firmly planted feet rest?
  But, where everything is as transparent and translucent
as the first day of your life, without apprehension, seeing as a revelation
  from one moment to another, washed in the rain.

DOVES

I hear the doves cooing
outside our window.

It is the softest of sounds
really.

That touches my skin
and begs to enter my body.

When it finally does, the softness of
their songs comes to rest

in each cell. And all the hardness
of life simply diffuses,

like my breath
into the air.

WORDS

Here, please
let me take these

words
out of your mouth

and
make something new

of them.
Do you ever

get tired of saying the same
words over and over again?

There is a newness within
us each, that we may discover

at any moment. You only have to
open your arms to let it all in.

As a sunflower opens up to the sun,
and follows its light,

from horizon to horizon,
across each day.

SEEING

What is seeing?
Do we believe without seeing,

or see because of a belief?
Does one come before the other?

Do you believe in the Mockingbird's
song, as it enters your heart?

Spinning out sutra after sutra, and binding
together with threads of light, every

constellation in the heavens. As each pupil draws
in that light, to reflect on the inner

surface of your eye's retina.
To become a sacrament of seeing.

THE TRAVELER

The mind is indeed a tremendous traveler,
it may skip from one universe to the next as

quickly as a passing thought, or focus its vision
tightly and fully on a single flower blooming

in the desert. Arising out of the emptiness
of all creation, in this present and

eternal moment of time, which is entirely
yours to discover, given as a gift from the heavens.

MOCKINGBIRD DANCES

This morning, I
    stand on our side porch

and look up at a Mockingbird
    that dances the dance only male

mockingbirds do so well. He is a daredevil –
    he jumps high, flaps his wings, then spins

twice in the air, to land lightly again and again,
    with (I promise you) such an expression of personal

delight and self satisfaction that something in me arises and
    wants to applaud, to say bravo, bravissimo, and to dance too!

DEATH

Listen, please,
we all know this is true

death comes at
some point

for us all.
But, haven't you

wondered what
part of yourself

will go on?
And what you may remember?

Will you remember your
tenth or eleventh or twelfth birthday?

Will you remember today,
as more than just another day?

Will you remember all the
precious moments of your life?

Look at someone you love today,
for one minute,

as if you saw them for
the first time.

As if they were the first ray
of sunlight, caught by

the tender passion of your eye,
lighting up your whole world.

*This poem calls out to Thornton Wilder's play **Our Town**, where Emily Webb remembers her twelfth birthday.*

Emily: Oh, Mama, look at me one minute as though you really saw me. Mama, fourteen years have gone by. I'm dead. You're a grandmother, Mama! Wally's dead, too. His appendix burst on a camping trip to North Conway. We felt just terrible about it - don't you remember? But, just for a moment now we're all together. Mama, just for a moment we're happy. Let's really look at one another!

[But no one took the time to look at one another. Finally, Emily responded in a moment of seemingly desperation and sadness. Once again speaking to the Stage Manager.]

...I can't. I can't go on. It goes so fast. We don't have time to look at one another. I didn't realize. So all that was going on and we never noticed. Take me back---up the hill to my grave.

But first: Wait! One more look. Good-by, Good-by, world. Good-by, Grover's Corners...Mama and Papa. Good-by to clocks ticking...and Mama's sunflowers. And food and coffee. And new ironed dresses and hot baths...and sleeping and waking up.

Oh, earth, you're too wonderful for anybody to realize you.

She looks toward the stage manager and asks abruptly, through her tears:

Do any human beings ever realize life while they live it? ---every, every minute?

Stage Manager: No. (pause) The saints and poets, maybe they do some.

NOT SUDDENLY AT ALL

It has come to me, not suddenly at all but
  slowly and perfectly throughout all the years
    that the heart is the first instrument of heaven.

And that if we are to see our own corner of the earth more
  clearly, then we must look at it through compassionate
  eyes, and listen in amazement with rare attention.

I know you have heard the song of Mockingbird, Dove,
  and Sparrow. Tell me, please, have you considered as me
    that their songs are bursting with the fullness of heaven?

NAMING A STAR

Do you know the story of starlight, of how it
  begins so far away that you cannot even dream
    from what corner of the heavens it travels from?

Take a deep breath, please, and try to imagine what
  it would feel like to travel from one still point to another
    as a continuous stream of light, as an angel of light.

On a journey, that begins at the farthest point away
  from earth, and then ends, striking on the inner surface of
    your eye, where the mind sees in it all the colors of creation.

If you were to go outside tonight and look up, what would
  you see? Would you tell the story of each star, floating there like
    vessels of light, waiting for someone to give each one a name?

Just like our ancestors once named all the constellations.
  If time is eternal, an illusion meaning nothing to you at all,
    could you easily take such a journey?

I think that I may, joyfully, like an angel of light,
  helping God to heal and perfect time and creation.

THE HEART CALLS OUT

what is belief, what is knowledge
do you know how to tell the difference

one from the other between the moments of desire
and the satisfaction of that desire

do you hear the bells of eventide ringing
through the soul, marking the time

do you hear the calling of
a stronger desire

we are meant to love, not just one
but many hearts across the years

the heart calls out again and again
as one desire fades

and another one arises
this is the gift life brings us

each and every day
the heart calls out, listen

LEAVENWORTH KANSAS

I was born here, close to
  the banks of the wild Missouri.
Which to me as a child was
  a massive brown and muddy beast,

a dark bear, mysterious in its desires,
  pawing its way step by step through
deep woods, unstoppable, defiant even.
  A force so strong and sure of itself,

it almost made me feel safe, in
  many ways it did. As a very small child,
my paternal grandfather
  (Grandpa, as I always knew him),

would bring me to play in this park, on
  a high bluff far above the Big Muddy.
Once when I was maybe four or nearly
  five, we marched across the old railroad bridge,

from Kansas to Missouri. How delighted
  we were, both with one another, as if we
had crossed into another country. We who were
  like Lewis and Clark, grand explorers.

I loved him dearly as he loved me, taking
  me with him to all his local haunts, the VFW Hall,
the American Legion. Where he always would
  order a tall cold beer,

and I in my turn a root beer. We
  were partners of conspiracy then, I knew
intuitively not to tell of our grand adventures,
  no one knew except the two of us in those days.

We were fearless together, the world to me was
  so big, and yet safe too. We walked as companions
of fate that fate could not begin to touch, our
  horizons boundless in possibilities.

OLD NICK

Ah Nick, you were the gentlest and caring of
  dogs and a skilled hunter of squirrels.
You are legend now, known in many circles,
  not because of your skills at running,

sniffing, and other dog mysteries,
  but because you had the warmest of hearts.
You who were a protector of children, how
  they all trusted and loved you instinctively.

I knew from the very beginning that we
  would be the best of friends, long before
your human mother and I were married.
  But, you my dear friend sealed the deal,

you were more than icing on the cake. You
  captured my heart and soul as much as
your mother did. In the old ways, it is between
  dogs and the family of man that goes back to

the very beginning. When humankind and dogkind first
  formed their ancient partnerships. Your heart was so gentle,
I remember one day when I was troubled at something,
  not trivial at all, and you knew.

You came and laid your gentle head in my lap,
  then looked up with such tenderness of spirit it simply
broke open my poor, tired heart to rest in the light.
  You were a balm of Gilead, an angel, a gift of God's grace.

As always suspected, I knew then and there that you were
  an old soul in a dog's body returned to teach me a measure
of love, of compassion, of kindness, even wisdom. You did that
  my old friend, you taught me that truth of unconditional love.

It's been many years now, and there is not a day or a week that
   goes by, when we don't pause to think of you. To dream that you
are out chasing squirrels, not as the renowned hunter you once
   were, but as a gentle playmate playing tag in the fields of heaven.

This is how we dream of you now, and more, much
   more. We suspect, you are now a most remarkable
angel of God, touching and healing hearts with
   compassion that knows no bounds.

As you once touched and healed ours, old friend.
   Your spirit, your memory lives within us your lessons
go on, in our remembrance, we honor the gift
   that you still are to us each.

SAINT JOHN'S CHURCH

In the countryside Northwest of the
town where my sister, a brother, and
I were born, (Leavenworth, Kansas)
towards Easton, Millwood, and Potter,

down a blue ribbon of long winding highway
with high rolling hills and several old
county roads of black top and fossilized
chert, stands a white wooden church,

my parents were married and
began their life together there
in September 1948.
American Gothic in style,

with peaked stain glass windows.
Over the years we have
(my whole family and I)
traveled this road so often,

I think that each one of us could
do so in our sleep, for some it
is still a place of dreams,
dreams from our childhood

and even beyond, becoming
a landscape that is laid out and
layered through our many memories.
So much so, that we can easily

close our eyes, and travel there again
and again, to St. John's Lutheran Church.
And the old family farm close by,
where we spent so many days

of our childhood,
running in the sun, playing
by the creek (catching crawdads to tease
my older sister with) that ran close

to the farmhouse where my grandparents
lived and raised a family of three.
My Uncle Leonard and Aunt Lois
were the most faithful couple

I ever knew, we ever knew.
They were like shining lights, pointing
out the loving way of relationships
and deep devotion, one to the other.

I can't imagine myself ever being so
humble, to have such humility of
the heart, that knows instinctively
how to love another with such

unconditional love and commitment.
It's been years now since they both passed
away, and still we remember and miss them,
sometimes with emptiness so deep

and so true, it brings loving tears to our eyes.
My Uncle Leonard was so gentle, with the
kindest of eyes, like my grandmother's, and
a smile that warmed your heart.

While his wife my Aunt Lois, was gaiety and
laughter itself with a twinkle in her eye (the
Irish would envy) and pure innocence,
which only added to her charm and personality.

My brother, two sisters, and I were their
only children, as were all their nieces
and nephews, and we loved them just as
they were perfect in their love for all of us.

St. John's is still there today, looking just as it did
the day our folks were wed, and my Mother's parents
before her. Laid to rest with many others,
on a high hillside, in a quiet place of peace.

St. John's is for all of us a place of pilgrimage,
where a welcome home is always known.
Where a connection to the land and sense
of a home is forever found and remembered.

Never to be forgotten, in this life, or the next.

Leonard Edward Meinert, 83, Leavenworth, Kansas, died Thursday, February 12, 2004, at Providence Medical Center, Kansas City, Kansas. He was born December 31, 1920, in Leavenworth Co., Kansas, the son of Edward John and Katherine Louise Wahaus Meinert. On November 10, 1945 he married Lois E. Emons at Easton, Kansas. She preceded him in death on November 6, 2000. Leonard worked for the Boss Glove Factory in Leavenworth for 14 years until it closed. He then worked for the McArthur School at Ft. Leavenworth, Kansas, from 1965 to 1986 until he retired. He was a member of the St. Paul Lutheran Church, Leavenworth, KS. He served 30 years on the St. Paul Lutheran Church finance committee. He is survived by his sister, Edna Starbuck, of Pasadena, TX. He was also preceded in death by his sister Frances Bottorff. Visitation will be held from 4 to 6 p.m. Sunday at the Davis Funeral Chapel. Funeral service will be held 10 a.m. Monday at the St. Paul Lutheran Church, the Rev. Ed Mease will officiate. Burial will be in the sunset Memory Gardens Cemetery. Memorial contributions may be given to St. Paul Lutheran Church, 7th and Miami Street, Leavenworth, Kansas 66048.

JUST AROUND THE CORNER

What I've learned to value most within
   this life, is that just around the corner of the

next moment, there is always something
   new to love. What did you see

today, like a shiny new penny in the
   eyes of child, that you have learned

to love? Where do you get your
   passion from? From what do you draw

your breath? If you haven't found it yet,
   I promise you, it's just around the next corner.

Pay Attention.

A QUAKER PRAYER

Let us pray, in stillness, in
silence, in sacred wonder
as the Friends do.

Entering into this place
of holiness, by turning thy
mind towards the light.

Sit quietly, in silence and in strength
while thee wait upon the Lord,
with a single heart and eye.

A single vision, filling thy body with light.

Let no other be present,
but the Lord, whose spirit is
waiting for thy company.

For God is spirit and truth,
and in spirit thou may worship
the Lord, waiting in the light.

Then let the next person enter
into this same place
with utter simplicity,

simplicity of the heart,
turning in thy mind as thee
have, in to the light.

Let thy heart and self be emptied,
waiting in thy spirit, in the spirit
that quiets all mortal flesh.

Where the oneness of God is found.

Letting all mortal flesh
keep silent in the
stillness of God.

Come nearer to thy Lord
than words may lead thee, to
know and simply,

the goodness of God.
Let thy silence become
an oblation to the Word,

a divine first step beyond
all emptiness, empty of
emptiness.

Where the oneness of thou,
O God, is known.

John 4:22-24 - "Woman, believe me, the hour is coming when you will worship the Father neither on this mountain nor in Jerusalem. You worship what you do not know; we worship what we know, for salvation is from the Jews. But the hour is coming, and is now here, when the true worshippers will worship the Father in spirit and truth, for the Father seeks such as these to worship him. God is spirit, and those who worship him must worship in spirit and truth."

This poem calls out to and responds to several Christian and Buddhist concepts and practices.

The first is a Quaker invocation written by Alexander Parker, in 1660, quoted from an article that also appeared in the Spring 2008 edition of *Parabola Magazine.*

The second is John 4:22-24, where Christ tells us that the true worshippers will worship the Father in spirit and truth, for God is spirit.

The third is this scripture Matthew 6:21-22 (21st Century King James Version): "For where your treasure is, there will your heart be also. The light of the body is the eye. If therefore thine eye be single, thy whole body shall be full of light."

The fourth is the ancient Eucharistic chant, Let all mortal flesh keep silence, based on verses taken from Habakkuk 2:20, "Let all the earth keep silence before Him."

And then last is the Buddhist concept of Śūnyatā or emptiness described in the Heart Sūtra. This quote comes from an exchange with the Rev. Cynthia Bourgeault a few years ago.

"I believe that nearly all spiritual experiences, as raw experience, occur in each tradition, but they are interpreted differently, according to different valuations of the states attained. By and large, Christianity does not assign definitive value to the state of emptiness itself, but places its emphasis on emptyING. States of profound emptiness are acknowledged in the most "avant-garde" of its mystical explorers, including Thomas Merton, Bernadette Roberts, and of course, Meister Eckhart. Merton, in his letter to Abdul Aziz (quoted in *Centering Prayer* and *Inner Awakening*), equates the state with the Islamic understanding of FANA, or self-annihilation.

Bernadette Roberts describes the state profoundly well but flatly (and aggressively) denies that it has anything to do with Śūnyatā. My take is that Christians, even at their mystical depths, tend to visualize this state as the ultimate gift of self, the ultimate oblation, rather than as a primordial ontological state. The map of the Christian universe begins with the Word, which in my estimation is the divine first step beyond emptiness." (Cynthia Bourgeault is an Episcopal Priest and author – who studied under Father Thomas Keating for many years and teaches now.)

THANKSGIVING MORNING

Today my life is a bit
   slower, no rushing about
      to run out the door and

into the traffic or to the office.
   With my morning coffee in hand, I walk
      through our yard, standing on each

porch, taking in all the morning
   sounds. The wind blows gently,
      and when it does the leaves above

appear to whisper their soft prayers
   to the morning. I wish I could teach you
      the words they use, the voice of leaf and limb,

but as you may clearly envision
   each tree speaks in its own language.
      In my case, I hear our neighbor's Pecan tree

praying for the squirrels racing up and
   down, tickling its bark, happy in that thought.
      And then our wise old Chinese Tallow

who meditates quietly in front of the
   house, our tall Sycamores at the side, where
      the Mockingbirds sing their favorite songs,

and then the Live Oaks from the park
   close by, each one has its own devotion
      to offer. I call them ours, even though

I know that they belong only to the earth
   and to God, who made them as we to belong
      to Him, who made every one of us.

Look up, and you will see
        many leaves still young and green,
                others just beginning to turn.

You know of course that as each
        single leaf falls that too is a prayer,
                a prayer of thanksgiving that echoes

in us each. Our thoughts colored
        by the words spoken, softly said,
                autumn comes you know to prepare

us for the stillness of winter.
        Winter of course is another kind
                of prayer spoken to the heart.

OUR BODIES KNOW HOW TO PRAY

It is with a stunning astonishing grace how
our own bodies know how to pray without
a second thought. Do you agree?

How our arms and legs and backs
know when to cross, when to genuflect,
bow low, and gently kneel, perfectly.

Bending our knees
down onto church pew
cushions for confession

and once again during Holy Communion,
before God's High Altar,
at just the right moment.

I love seeing the faces of
God's people as they come before
His presence during Eucharist,

for this moment of grace
and love as I love seeing
His people holding

up their open hands
and hearts, to accept the wafer,
the Body of Christ.

And then the wine,
His cup of salvation
offered each service.

I love especially the faces of
the children, knowing that
one day soon

they too will stand where
I am standing, to offer me this
same sacrament.

As Christ offers Himself, in love
to each of us again and again,
this is the yoga of Jesus.

And how this whole act
is one of remembrance, to help us
each remember that we are His.

To remember His two greatest commandments,
the first exactly like the second, thus we are
reminded to love one another and the

Lord God above. They are all moments of
epiclesis, where we are each touched and healed
by the Holy Spirit, God's divine presence.

Who is always with us, who is
always at work in the world,
God who is both noun and verb.

PERICHORESIS

As thou dwellest in Christ
  and as Christ dwells
in thee, may ye dwell
  in one another too.

Let your indwelling be
  an intimacy in which
ye may breathe
  together. In meditation

as one finishes one
  breath, let the other
follow thee in breathing,
  so that in breathing

in and breathing out,
  your breaths will match.
Let this be a cleaving
  together, where ye

through Christ are joined
  as one, in one body.
Where each breath ye
  breathe together

becomes the breath of
  God, sustaining all
creation in the mystery
  of the Incarnation.

As Christ pours himself
  into thee, let thou
do the same for all
  thy neighbors.

This is the dance
  of being and
becoming, of
  giving and receiving.

It is the dance of
  creation itself, where
thou, O Lord, pourest
  out all thy blessings

upon the mortal flesh
  of humankind, and
where thou as thyself, through
  love, redeemest thy reign.

Thy kingdom surely
  comes, thy will
be done, on earth
  as in thy highest heaven.

"That they all may be one; as thou, Father, art in me, and I in thee, that they also may be one in us (John 17:21)."

TO MARY OLIVER AT ADVENT

Reading one of your poems is like
opening a gift before Christmas.

It is magical, wonder filled,
but more than that too.

Each word and verse flowing through
the mind elicits something deep inside me,

and before I know it words of
my own begin

to land lightly onto a blank page, this page.
What does Christmas teach us, you think?

I think forgiveness first, and that God
in his eternal judgment, will never judge

us harsher than we have already judged
ourselves. If Christmas means anything

at all, it means this. It gives birth to a
compassion that flows throughout all creation.

And so, we each must come to our own nativity,
where God's love for the world is born.

Where we learn to cradle Christ in the heart,
learn to change our life, even the world.

Your own world.

The final lines of this poem are an allusion to Mary Oliver's poem "Swan," from her book of poems by that name. As well, she tells us in her notes, the last sentence in Rainer Maria Rilke's poem "Archaic Torso of Apollo."

THE ZEN IN ALL OF US

the soundless sound
the cupless cup
the breathless breath

the fearful hero
the loving heart
the painless pain

the invisible sutra
the silent whisper
the sweetest strawberry

the dancing thought
the lovely legs
the Buddha Smiles

i have said enough, for
now, poetry brings out
the Zen in all of us

The Buddha-Dharma arises from difficulty, the more difficult the better. - Master Hsuan Hua

THE PERFECTION OF WISDOM - HEART SUTRA

How often have you wondered,
  as did the Buddha, as I have many times
before, between each moment
  of desire, and each

desire found within the hollow yearnings
  and attachments of the heart, the answer
to this question? What is the perfection of
  wisdom, when will it come?

If all things are empty, simply beyond or outside
  our every single memory, beyond thought and feeling,
beyond all willfulness of mind and consciousness.
  Where will you find yourself then?

Beyond all our senses of seeing and
  believing. Beyond our bodies, that
smell and touch, our tongues that taste
  and speak, our ears that often find no

rest in silence. Beyond all conceptions
  of the mind and self, where fear fades
away, emptied by the self. Beyond all
  grief and guilt that may distort the heart.

Where will you find yourself then? When
  all imagination and suffering ceases and
you awaken from the dream of life, where
  alpha and omega are one, where loss vanishes.

Where compassion teaches us an
  interconnectedness to one another,
that neither increases nor decreases,
  which is changeless and changing.

Where all sense of self dissolves
   away as we welcome the embrace
of heaven found in a single moment
   between breathing in and out.

Where God is known as a oneness
   and compassion, the single one who unwinds
and heals the sleeping self, to awaken
   within us the single heart of love.

SORROWS OF THE HEART (FOR JULIA)

There are times, like today, when
　my heart is so full of grief that it
seems to take on all the sorrow and
　despair that is at work in this world.

When it does, when I feel like this,
　it is as if my soul has shattered and
spread out into uncounted pieces,
　scattered across all creation,

into the far-flung corners of one universe
　after another, which are too remote and
too numerous to be found.
　Please listen to me in such a moment;

the only thing that I can positively do is to
　offer such sorrow as a prayer and
sacrifice up to heaven. Where God,
　who always listens, who always knows,

who has already heard each single word
　and thought my heart has ever uttered.
Who in response sends angels
　and archangels, into every corner

you may imagine, to gather there
　like seeds of brilliant light, the shattered
shards of my heart, back into my being.
　This of course is what love does, it pieces together

a broken heart and heals the world.
　The wise person knows that such sorrow
is a gift, a gift marked by compassion. It is
　more than that; it is you helping creation

to heal the world, you my friend were made
　for that you know. Yes, we were each made
for this you know. You know this too; it
　is written in the hidden places of our hearts.

COMPUNCTIONS OF THE MIND

In our childhood years, down pathways
only half remembered are compunctions
of the mind, and penitent hearts
marked by an undying conscience.

You may have your own sorrows and regrets
to cleanse. Years ago as a small boy of
nine or ten, I owned a wooden slingshot.
Given to me, perhaps as

a birthday present from an Aunt or an
Uncle, or even something I had saved
(Gladly would I pay it all back now Seventy times
Seven.) my nickels and dimes up to buy.

I can remember learning how to hold
it strongly in my left hand held up
high, where the handle met the
shape of the 'Y' to frame any target.

As children we practiced hitting tin cans
at first, perfecting our form and accuracy
to a 'T', learning how to sight down
the edge of one side,

how to pull back on the latex bands
as far as we could pull, how to aim
and then release, to fire it like a gun
and hit the target squarely.

How terribly delighted we were,
when our BBs and pellets hit the can,
penetrating through the tough sides
and knocking it off fence or wall.

I can remember so clearly, to my
dishonor even today, how I stood
at the bottom of a tree looking up
at a singing Robin sitting on a branch.

Standing quietly, breathing in slowly
and then deliberately taking aim, pulling
back as far as it would go;
Ready, Aim, and Fire.

Death came as such as surprise, suddenly, and
Oh, so sadly; there was no moment of
celebration, just emptiness and a sense of loss
where once was life, now nothing.

Life cut shorter than it should be
by the thoughtless act of a small
young boy, wishing only to do valiant
and heroic things within the world.

Listen carefully, the only thing
I know to do now is to love
that little boy with my whole
heart, pouring all the kindness

and love that I can find into the sorrow of
his broken heart and being, and taking his
pain and regret into my own heart,
like practicing Tonglen as the Buddhists do.

To ask for forgiveness, practicing again
and again, the taking of suffering
and sending of compassion, in the hope
"all shall be well

and all manner of thing
shall be well." Sin is "behovable"
as St. Julian reveals to us,
it "plays a needful part."

Thus, led through life, we walk
down a path once known and never
fully forgotten, intimately sought,
held in God's highest esteem.

Sin is "behovable," since God's infinite mercy
offers us a closing word, an absolution if you will
and a blessing, even one when it is unasked for,
freely given by Christ from the cross.

Christ who has paid the price not once, but
many times over for my sins. Christ holds
him now that small, young boy, who still
sheds tears, years and years later

for the life of a gentle Robin, whom I hope
sings a song of forgiveness, even now,
forever now, in the stillness of
a single human heart.

L'CHAYIM
to life – to liberty – to truth

People will say most anything!

They come along calling President Obama a Hitler talking from
both sides of their mouth. Where do they get all
this talk from, I ask an old friend?

Now leaning more than a bit towards the right. I like a man who
speaks his mind, and lets you know what he's thinking, an open
and honest opinion shared is critical to any democracy.

But to be fair, there is no comparison
or truth in what they offer or say in this,
they are far off the mark my old friend.

And this I know is not you my friend
it never has been and it never will be

Where are the concentration camps, where are the
death camps, where are the six million plus dead Jews,
the Freemasons who died for tolerance, for freedom,
the gays and the lesbians who were persecuted and then
experimented on.

All the children of Auschwitz who labored and died, for what.
And the other camps too, Buchenwald, Dachau, Bergen-Belsen.
Can you name them all, memorize each name
(1,200 camps and sub camps)?

All told, counted by some, at twenty one million dead
in a democide, genocide, politicide, and mass murder
unimaginable today.

Where are the Gypsies and their children? Only two
survived at Auschwitz. Did they know that? I doubt they did.

How dare they compare that which they know nothing of obviously
now, or have forgotten, lost in fear - fed on a diet of - fear and
intolerance.

And this I know is not you my friend
it never has been and it never will be

What the hell do they know of "The Shoah" anyway?
They know nothing of this word, this history. I tell you my
brothers and sisters and family died there in that time and place.

Go ahead and let them get angry all they want - split a gut open
for all I care with their hatred and myth making. But at some point,
somewhere some poet or writer is going to tell it true.

And then they will mourn at their own shame if they will see it,
own it for what it is and how they helped a great nation fall into
fear and spread that fear even further.

And this I know is not you my friend
it never has been and it never will be

We are all equal in God's fine sight, we are all his children.
America is as much about taking care of its own, than some in
Congress or the media, or some of the poor bankers and board
room executives on Wall Street might have you believe.

Where I've been more than once myself, they too are Americans,
and many see it right - they know the difference.

But, until some people know their history until they know the true
difference between capitalism and socialism, between death and
living - truly living.

And stop using them as trigger words to manipulate some poor
girl working in a "Dime Store" or "Wal-Mart" or some such place
at minimum wage, or a poor person living only on Social Security.

These good Americans might want to open a newspaper or a history
book, or an economics book first, and read and read again, and then
learn something more from reading, than all this garbage they are
spilling out now in the name of America.

And this I know is not you my friend
it never has been and it never will be

Stop and think, please, that at least one half the people or more in this great nation, don't see it their way. And, thank God, they never will, which makes us stronger as a nation. When you look back and see where we all came from, it wasn't from this landscape?

Although we have made it our own, the farmers, the ranchers, the bakers, the builders, the dreamers, even the immigrant ditch diggers.

My ancestors have been here since nearly the beginning, 1680 or so, long before the first American Revolution and by God you can't tell me that this is why they came; this America that they say is without hope, that lives in fear.

Because that is what I hear in all these words and blubbering, no hope: a world and a nation without hope, a world of fear. And some keep buying into it seems.

And this I know is not you my friend
it never has been and it never will be

And if they knew anything of history, they would know, this is exactly how Hitler and his "Bullies" and "Brown Shirts" manipulated his own people and scared them into killing the Jews, the Gypsies, the mentally disabled. The Christians, like Dietrich Bonheoffer who spoke up in truth. It was Hitler's own voice of FEAR that took them all in that direction, and I hear echoes of it today from the far right.

The talk show hosts with their rhetoric of fear.

And this I know is not you my friend
it never has been and it never will be

And while we are at it, we might remember, with great reverence
that there were decent men and women in the world, like our

own fathers and mothers. Good people who rose up in World War
Two and fought to end such hatred and killing.

"Is the wish to kill never killed?"

It seems not in all their angry words, the killing is going on still
and then there is the shame, the deep, abiding shame
in embracing a hopelessness beyond all knowing.

By not knowing or loving, by forgetting whom we are
as people, as Americans.

And this I know is not you my friend
it never has been and it never will be

FALL HAS FINALLY COME

I

Fall has finally come, no longer
 do we hear the long, sultry symphony
 of the cicada that I always

miss as the warmest days
 lengthen into Indian Summer.
 Our days grow shorter; the sunlight

noticeably softens and dims, colors change,
 our breathing shares a gentle touch of
 winter flowing through the

crisp autumn air. The early evening
 light has turned with time, to
 early morning, the sun sets

sooner and rises sooner too.
 I welcome the nighttime's
 cover, its darkness a blanket

that I may wrap myself in
 for comfort, or an old friend
 who comes to our fireside

for a long and deep soulful
 conversation. While sipping on
 a generous thirty year old scotch,

that seems more than meet this
 time of the year, perfect for a cold
 fall evening.

II

I have two best friends, who stood by me at
　our wedding as I once did at theirs. Such is
　our history and long friendships that

we know more about each other,
　than we may wish others to see,
　still, our deepest secrets safe.

Our stories have passed into
　the realm of legend and lore,
　myth and fable,

magic and enchantment, our lives rich
　in metaphor and tall Texas tales. Do you
　remember when, we ask one another?

And we do, we do remember.
　There are moments, like now,
　when I miss their laughter and

lively humor, the easy commerce
　of their company, when nothing else
　is expected, except to be together.

Even, though the wild and mostly
　brilliant days of our youth,
　which were never truly wasted

may be gone now, like kindred spirits,
　we will always share a fellowship of
　manhood.

III

My most humble wish this evening, is to
  enjoy the warm circle of our closeness
  again. Where we raise a glass or two in a

toast to life that washes all our cares and
  grief away, the burdens that may bear
  down upon our souls.

Time turns, again, we have traveled
  this pathway before together,
  in many places, across lives

and livelihoods that stretch back
  beyond our subtle human memory,
  bound as we are to the goodness

of this earth. And yet, there is wisdom
  and learning that has grown within
  us each, one which sees beyond

all sorrow in this life. Wisdom that
  sees through the darkest veil into
  the light of God's

eternal love,
  fully known, tied as we are to
  His mystery and myth.

Psalm 133
A Song of Ascents. Of David.

1 *Behold, how good and how pleasant it is*
    For brethren to dwell together in unity!

2 *It is like the precious oil upon the head,*
    Running down on the beard,
    The beard of Aaron,
    Running down on the edge of his garments.

3 *It is like the dew of Hermon,*
    Descending upon the mountains of Zion;
    For there the LORD *commanded the blessing—*
    Life forevermore.

THE PERSON WHO IS AWAKE

The Person Who Is Awake
has conquered the world.
How can they lose the way
who are beyond the way?

Like Christ and the Buddha,
like all enlightened people,
their eyes are open and
their feet are free.

Who can follow after them?
The world will not claim them
or lead them astray, nor the poisoned
nets of desire hold them.

They are awake. They are awake.
They find joy in the stillness of prayer,
contemplation, and meditation and in
sweet surrender to the Lord of Hosts.

They seek the highest consciousness.
They are free from fear. They are free to live.
They live in joy and in love.
They find their joy in love.

They live in compassion and loving-kindness.
They look within and are still.
They become still to know the Lord
and are renewed with a right spirit.

They are still, and know the Lord.
They are exalted with humility.
The Lord of hosts is with them.
They find refuge in the Lord.

They are washed clean, whiter
than snow. Their flesh and bones,
once broken, are made whole.
Behold, they have found

Thy truth in the deepest and inward
places of themselves. Through these
hidden places they have come to know
Thy wisdom.

With a quiet mind
they open their hearts to compassion
feeling the joy of the Lord's way.
They are delivered.

They are saved, and sing aloud
of Thy righteousness Lord.
Their broken hearts and spirits
are healed and made whole.

They rejoice. They rejoice.
Because they have seen the Truth
of Thy word, from the very beginning of time.
They rejoice, in seeking your pleasure Lord.

They arise. They arise.
And all about them the earth changes.
Compassion rules their actions.
Their hearts are open to one another.

They abide in love and
are known by the Lord.
They help to heal the earth
and to restore

Thy people to Thy ways.
They have found that we are one.
They have discovered we are all
Thy people.

They rejoice in righteousness and
offer themselves before Thy holy altar.
Thy Holy Spirit dwells once again
within Thy people.

These verses are based on an interpretation of scriptures and translations taken from both the Old Testament Psalms (46, 48, 51) and the Dhammapada (14, 15, 26) one of the earliest masterpieces of Buddhist literature, ascribed to the Buddha himself. It is surprisingly easy to combine verses and ideas from these two sacred scriptures. This is essentially what I did by reading each one back and forth, which was part of the creative process. Some verses are wholly new, ones I added, inspired you might say by the Holy Spirit, or at least by my seeing how closely they align to one another.

There are several different sources and translations of both the Psalms and the Dhammapada found on the internet. For the Psalms, I used the 21st Century King James Version found on the BibleGateway.com site. Verses related to the Dhammapada drew heavily upon the 1993 translation completed by Thomas Byrom, which I found to be the most appealing, straightforward and easiest to read for a Western mind

In exploring both Abrahamic (Judeo-Christian-Islamic) and Buddhist concepts about God and the divine, many scholars will agree that they each conceptualize God quite differently. They all begin in different places, within a specific historical, linguistic, and cultural context across thousands of years. As the world we know today grows smaller and smaller and as ideas fly at the speed of light across the internet, we are all challenged to re-imagine our relationship with the divine and one another in new ways. Many people believe that God is changeless, and I would agree that this may indeed be true, but it also seems that creation itself is constantly changing as is one moment from the next. In many ways, as theologian Paul F. Knitter suggests in his book "Without Buddha I Could not be a Christian" we may now begin to see "God as a Verb", actively pouring out the Holy Spirit across creation, moving as a Connecting Spirit in and with and through creation which is still expanded, still in progress, still evolving and calling us into relationship with one another. If God is endless, has "no end", is "unending", in which "there is no end"; if God is boundless, has no "boundaries; " if God is "ineffable; " if God is more than the Alpha and the Omega of all creation; is not all of creation and how creation is changing, also contained within God?

I have intentionally used the word Lord, instead of God in the verses since the word Lord seems more intimate to me and can be widely applied to different religious and cultural concepts about the mystery of God and the path to enlightenment and salvation. But, in nearly all cases it also refers to a meaning of a monotheistic God, as Abba, as Father, as in the Lord God Almighty, and the Lord of Hosts to put it into a more traditional Abrahamic (Judeo-Christian-Islamic) form of thought. Still, as a word as a specific image of the Ultimate Divine Mystery, it is a finger pointing at the moon, but one I hope that points us toward an intimate loving relationship.

TONGLEN FOR NEWTOWN
(Now I Lay Me Down To Sleep)

You have known this one
prayer by memory since
you were a child,
it's a good place to start.

"Now I lay me down to
sleep if I should die
before I wake, I pray
the lord my soul to take."

There are times
like this,
when you just have
to stop doing

whatever you are doing
and simply pray.
Practice some tonglen,
like the Buddhist do

or light a candle
as a Christian does
in church, kneeling
before some sacred altar.

Tonglen is the taking of another's
pain and the giving of love.
We begin by taking on
the suffering

of a person we
know to be hurting, of
the world even as Christ did,
and whom we wish to help.

This takes the greatest
compassion; it is breathing in
all the darkness.
And then letting the love

of your heart turn it
instantly into the light
of a billion stars and suns,
and then breathing out

again all that love
into the world,
the light brightening
the world, turning

it again and again.
It's true you know,
love makes
the world go round,

even when, perhaps
especially when it
has stopped making
all sense. This is when

we need such
prayers
and praying
the most.

WHEN ANGELS ARE BORN

There is an old Jewish parable, I once read
of two friends, long separated
by years and distance.

The story goes, that once
they were reunited, an angel
was born, an angel of friendship.

This is more than common knowledge in heaven,
but on earth a secret of sorts for some reason,
let it be a secret no more.

We give birth to angels all the time,
when a child smiles at you in innocent
wonder for the world,

with that curious look only they can give,
a bright new angel is born, let us name her
an angel of wonderment.

When a mother picks up
her child, hurt by some awkward fall
and with caring love soothes the pain

and wipes the tears away, another
new angel is born, let us name him
the angel of compassion.

Whenever a stranger is given
aid, they may be homeless or not,
an angel of mercy is born.

When a Mockingbird's song touches
your ears with the brightest notes
to remind you

that music moves throughout
all the heavens of creation, then a
symphony of angels is born.

The world is full of such angels,
you give birth to them every day
without even knowing.

Can you begin to imagine
what changes, in the world,
you can make yourself

by fully realizing that each
thought and deed is an
angel in the making?

And can you imagine further
still, how this changes
your own world?

Is it any wonder, that
both Christ and the Buddha
told us to be lights of the world.

Let your mind become a light
and let your heart shine
with the light of love.

To make of ourselves a light.

Matt. 5:14-16 'You are the light of the world. A city built on a hill cannot be hidden. No one after lighting a lamp puts it under the bushel basket, but on the lamp stand, and it gives light to all in the house. In the same way, let your light shine before others, so that they may see your good works and give glory to your Father in heaven."

In his final words under the Sala trees, the Buddha gave us these words. "Make of yourself a light."

All who find freedom from clinging to desire, sin, separation, and sorrow, free from the incessant flow of their thoughts, are like shining lights reaching final liberation in the world. - The Dhammapada 89

AFTERWORD

Poets and writers have long been inspired by the sacred literature of the world's religions and faiths, with stories of wisdom, transformation, enlightenment, and salvation. The word literature points us towards the high art of communicating ideas, feelings, beliefs and wisdom through writing, of thoughts made with letters. Poets are storytellers who use letters and language, myth and metaphor, as symbols to communicate with the world. The language they use may be both literal and emblematic, expressing the inexpressible and ineffable through images, narrative, emotion, and truth that open us up to the mystery of life.

Some of the greatest literature written across human history comes from the sacred scriptures and mythologies of the world; from the Hindu Mahabharata and Ramayana to the Bible's Old and New Testament; the Celtic-Welsh Mabinogion and Celtic-Erin Cath Maige Tuired; Ancient Greek and Egyptian Mythology; or the Dhammapada and Heart Sutra of Buddhism. Our sacred scriptures and ancient mythologies hold the stories and narratives of our relationship with one another, the universe, and the Ultimate Divine Mystery of creation, with God. And the journey we take to free ourselves from the tyranny of our own minds, the struggle to see truly what is real and our own unique place in the world. Poetry helps us to believe and know that we are part of something greater than what we may imagine as our soul struggles to find meaning in this life, to know and be known by this greater mystery, and fully embrace our unlimited potential to love within creation.

Many of the poems in *When Angels Are Born* draw upon the spiritual traditions and language found in Christianity, Buddhism, Hinduism and other contemplative wisdom traditions and faiths. Poetry as a language calls us into an intimate relationship with one another, the divine, and creation that is ultimately transforming; poetry is also a celebration of life, a call to live life fully with a full awareness of life's value. My hope as a poet is that these poems will help the reader to see more clearly, to offer some clarity to your own vision of life and sense of self, and how your life, the self, the soul, or the human psyche are constantly changing and evolving through all your relationships, through love. And that life, your own life especially is indeed a divine gift of love, however, you may imagine the divine to be at work within the world, your world.

"The Lord bless thee and keep thee; the Lord make His face shine upon thee, and be gracious unto thee; the Lord lift up His countenance upon thee, and give thee peace." - Numbers 6:24-26 (21st Century King James Version)

ABOUT THE AUTHOR

Ron Starbuck has been deeply engaged in an Interfaith-Buddhist-Christian dialogue for many years. He holds a lifelong interest in Christian mysticism, comparative religion, theology, and various forms of contemplative practice. He is the author of *When Angels Are Born,* his second collection of poetry found within these pages, and *Wheels Turning Inward,* his first collection of poetry. Each collection follows a poet's mythic and spiritual journey that crosses easily onto the paths of many contemplative traditions.

He is also the Chief Executive Officer of Saint Julian Press, Inc., a new nonprofit imprint, and a former Vice President with J.P. Morgan Chase, now serving in the public sector on an information technology, executive management team.

Forming a nonprofit press to work with emerging and established writers and poets, and tendering new introductions to the world at large in the framework of an interfaith and cross cultural literary dialogue has been a long time dream. He has written occasionally for *Parabola Magazine* and from time to time author's an interfaith dialogue blog on the Saint Julian Press web site.

http://saintjulianpress.com/index.html

ACKNOWLEDGMENTS

I am deeply grateful to my wife Joanne, to her ongoing patience, love, understanding, and passionate support, and to the intimacy of spirit we have discovered in our life together. Her gentle presence and spirit flows throughout these poems.

To my parents Robert and Edna Starbuck, who introduced me to some of the greatest literature, poets, and writers of humankind. They opened my heart and eyes to a world of storytelling, sacred works, infinite human possibilities, compassion, awe and wonder.

In gratitude to close and intimate friends, both near and far, who keep me humble and have helped me to see clearly the transforming value in writing and sharing these poems. You have given me both courage and encouragement at many hidden levels of the self, you have touched my spirit as we have touched one another's spirit.

And to all the great writers and poets who have inspired this work. Especially authors Hélène Cardona, Paul F. Knitter, and Laurence Freeman who very graciously provided eloquent endorsement quotes (blurbs).

Gracious thanks to *Parabola Magazine*, and Executive Editor - Tracy Cochran who courageously reached out to me on two separate occasions to submit and include Tangents (book reviews/interviews) in the pages of *Parabola*. One with author and professor, Paul F. Knitter of Union Theological Seminary in Manhattan, and the other with Fr. Laurence Freeman, author and director of the World Community for Christian Meditation. Their work as teachers and authors has influenced many of the poems in *When Angels Are Born*, and *Wheels Turning Inward* a previous book of poetry.

A truly memorable and grateful thank you to Melissa Studdard, English Professor at Lone Star College, and author of *Six Weeks to Yehidah*, who helped open several literary doors, and interviewed me for *Tiferet Journal's* blog talk radio program, *Tiferet Talk*.

The poem "Park Avenue" first appeared in The Criterion: An International Journal in English, December 2011, Volume II - Issue IV. *http://www.the-criterion.com/V3/n1/Poetry.pdf*

The poem "Mockingbird Dances" first appeared in *Tiferet Journal*, in the Fall 2012 issue. Special thanks go out to poetry editor Adele Kenny, for her gracious help in navigating their submission process.

The poems "There Are Times", "Whenever You Watch Me", "The Monarch", "Storm Shadow", "Park Avenue", "Sandburg and Monroe", and "Austin David Meek" first appeared through Saint Julian Press, published online. "Sandburg and Monroe" uses literary allusion to draw upon the poetic writing style and vocabulary of Carl Sandburg. You will see this easily if you know and love Sandburg's work.

The poem "Whenever You Watch Me", is a literary response or another allusion to one originally written by E.E. Cummings, "somewhere i have never traveled, gladly beyond". We learn from the master poets who come before us all.

The poem "Perichoresis", first appeared in *Mark Miller's One-Volume 9-Wheels Turning Inward, [Kindle Edition]*, where all the proceeds are donated to Give Kids the World, a charitable organization where children with life-threatening illnesses and their families are treated to weeklong, cost-free fantasy vacations.

The poem "The Buddha Speaks", was inspired by the *Burning World,* Spring 2012 edition of *Parabola Magazine*, "The Fire Sermon" translation.

The poem "Compunctions of the Mind", uses an allusion from Saint Julian of Norwich's *Sixteen Revelations of Divine Love* (circa 1393). Julian of Norwich, is considered to be one of the greatest English mystics, very little is known of her life aside from her writings. Her mystical visions were the source of this major work, which is believed to be the first book written by a woman in the English language.

CHAPTER XXVII - CHAPTER XXVII

"Often I wondered why by the great foreseeing wisdom of God the beginning of sin was not hindered: for then, methought, all should have been well. Sin is behovable—[playeth a needful part]—; but all shall be well

But Jesus, who in this Vision informed me of all that is needful to me, answered by this word and said: It behoved that there should be sin; (Synne is behovabil) but all shall be well, and all shall be well, and all manner of thing shall be well.

(56) And for the tender love that our good Lord hath to all that shall be saved, He

comforteth readily and sweetly, signifying thus: It is sooth (i.e. truth, an actual reality) that sin is the cause of all this pain; but all shall be well, and all shall be well, and all manner [of] thing shall be well."

The poem "When Angels Are Born", was inspired by the *Friendship - Companions on the Path*, Winter 2004 edition of *Parabola Magazine*, epicycles - traditional stories from around the world "The Angel of Friendship", Jewish.

The poem "L'Chayim" calls out to the work of Carl Sandburg and his style of writing. As an allusion, it draws upon the essence of his poems *To a Contemporary Bunkshooter*, *The People, Yes*, and other works by Sandburg. It also draws on Arthur Miller's play, *After The Fall*, "my brother's died here", "is the wish to kill never killed?"

After the Fall, was first performed in the Lincoln Center Repertory Company, New York City, on January 23, 1964. The action takes place in the mind, thought, and memory of Quentin, many say this is Arthur Miller and Maggie was Marilyn Monroe, his former wife.

I first heard Miller's work presented as a child in one of my father's sermons; the play touched me deeply then and still does today. "We must understand that often life begins only after a moment of despair and even destruction, after we have reached the very depth of hell, after, after the Fall. So it is with the play throughout and as it comes to the end. Maggie has died of an overdose. Quentin is searching for his own being in the midst of this tragic death and the death of all those who died in the concentration camps."

He speaks to Holga, one of the characters in the play, but he seems to be speaking to all of us. Quentin speaks: *"But love, is love enough? What love, what weave of pity will ever reach this knowledge---I know how to kill?...I know, I know—she was doomed in any case, but will that cure? Or is it possible---He turns toward the tower, moves toward it as toward a terrible God—that this is not bizarre...to anyone? And I am not alone, and no man lives who would not rather be the sole survivor of this place than all its finest victims! What is the cure? Who can be innocent again on this mountain of skulls? I tell you what I know! My brothers died here--- He looks from the tower down to the fallen Maggie.*
...And that, that's why I wake each morning like a boy---even now, ever now! I swear to you, I could love the world again! It's the knowing all? To know, and even happily, that we meet unblessed; not in some garden of wax fruit and painted trees, that lie of Eden, but after, after the Fall, after many, many deaths. Is the knowing all? And the wish to kill is never killed, but with some gift of courage one may look into its face when it appears, and with a stroke of love---as to an idiot in the house—forgive it; again and again...forever?"

www.ingramcontent.com/pod-product-compliance
Lightning Source LLC
Chambersburg PA
CBHW051837040426
42447CB00006B/573